Life style

By

Jakeline Bryant

COPYRIGHT© 2016

BY

Jakeline Bryant

This book or any portion thereof may

not be reproduced or used in any

manner whatsoever without the

express written permission of the

publisher except for the use of brief

quotations in a book review.

Introduction

Tiny home living is a decision that some people are hesitant to make. For one, the society has this certain standard when it comes to houses, which involves preference for big ones. Very few people aspire to live in a tiny home.

Finding new ways to store things isn't always an easy thing to do. If you have a small house and a lot of stuff you've probably already found yourself struggling to make the most out of every space and you're probably still swimming in extra stuff right? Well the first step is going to be going through what you already have and make sure that you have the space for everything as well as having a way to organize it all.

Very few know people; living in a tiny home has a lot of advantages. In fact, it is slowly becoming one of the trends in some countries where space comes at a very high price like the United States and Japan.

If you are planning to make the move from big to small, there are a lot of things that you should first be aware of. This book offers a *proven guide* towards living small including *tips and techniques* on how you can organize and design your tiny home space. Just try to learn as much as possible and you're off to a good start.

Who this book for

1. Planning to build tiny house.
2. People who are looking to downsizing.
3. Who already have tiny house but struggling to make most out of it.
4. People who are looking to customize their house for maximum space.
5. People who are looking for effective and artistic living.
6. People who want to make their limited floor space look more spacious.
7. People who are looking for successful tiny house living.

"If you are looking for answer, to one of these question than you came to right place".

Table of contents

Introduction

Chapter-1

The Tiny House Lifestyle

Actual space you have to work with

Number of divisions you intend your home to have

Purpose for your move

Things you can bringing with you

House theme

Light and ventilation

Building and zoning laws

Durable materials

Number of people to be accommodated

Chapter- 2

Benefits of Tiny House Lifestyle

Lesser cost

Reduced carbon footprint

Low maintenance

Bare essentials

Personal space for single people

Mobility

Be more in control of your life – particularly your finances

More resources

A wiser lifestyle

Environment and energy

Emergency and conversion housing

Homelessness

The economy and development

Zoning law blockades and benefits

Big benefits of tiny houses

Chapter-3

Financial Aspect of Tiny House Lifestyle

How Much Will a Tiny House Cost?

How to Save Money on Your Tiny House Construction?

Build It Yourself

Select Your Building Materials Well

Be Resourceful/Get Creative

Chapter -4

Organizing: The Basic Principle of Tiny House Lifestyle

Decluttering

Planning

Proper Motivation

Chapte-5

The Entrance

Chapter-6

Storage

Maximize those Closets

Use Vertical Dividers

Utilize the Area under the Stairs

Create a Mudroom Bench

Stack them below

Go Minimalist with Your Living Room Furniture

Build Over-door or Over-Window Shelves

Add Zen to a Work Den

Versatile Ottoman Chairs

Chapter-7

Living Room

Choose sofas on raised legs

Put on mirrors that will reflect the view outside

Keep things minimal

Avoid bulky chairs

Do not go too big on paintings

Have foldable seats instead of bean bags

Board-less sofas

Add a piece or two of small indoor plants

Choose chair/sofas will small arms

Go for a wall-mounted flat screen TV

Shelves

The Bookshelf

Wall Cabinet

Ottoman

Toy Chest

Chapter-8

Kitchen

Smart Kitchen Storage

Don't Compromise an Open Floor Plan

Keep Trash Out of Sight

Build an Island

Utilize the Corners

The Cabinets

The Pantry

The Fridge

Wall Hanging Pot Rack

Utensil Rack

Baskets

Boxes

Toe Kick

Add Levels

Chapter-9

Dining Room

Opt for glass tables

Allot moving space for chairs from the dining table

Avoid chairs with tall/huge backrests

Go for tables with a detachable leaf

Consider getting a round table

Armless dining chairs

China Cabinet/Hutch

Pantry

Chapter-10

Bedroom

Cleaning up your closet

Do not put in beds that are too large

Keep the room as open as possible

Go for bold designs

Maximize every inch of space

Put on artworks

Do away with the conventional

Try to get ideas from the internet

Add a multifunctional bedside table

Add a touch of your own style

Don't Forget the Drawers

Consider a Day Bed

Maximize the Wall Space

Hide Items that are Rarely Used

Set Up a Home Office in Your Closet

Make Every Furniture and Accessory Piece Count

Organizing the Kids Room

Use Bunk Beds for the Kids' Room

Chapter-11

Bathroom

Use Pastel Colors

Use a Glass Door

Use Indirect Lighting

Provide Natural Light to the Bathroom

Maximize the Wall Space

Space Savers

Baskets

Laundry Hamper

Large Sink

Chapter-12

Maximizing: The Ultimate Goal of Tiny House Lifestyle

Create Focal Walls

Mount Mirrors for Depth

Lighten Up the Area

Swing-arm Sconces Free Up Some Space

Open the Area Up

Keep Every Area Clean and Clutter Free

Use a Single Color Palette

Create Different Zones

Use Multipurpose Furniture

Essential Tips

Chapter-13

Successful Tiny House Living

Be organized.

Use curtains that are the same color as the walls

Have an open source for natural light

Bring outside colors inside

Put on the same color for adjacent spaces

Use neutral background and light colors

Go for less furniture

Add a floor-ceiling book shelf, but do not fill it

Avoid too much detail

Have some large mirrors in the room

Use striped carpet

Schedule a décor display rotation

Examine the traffic flow

Keeping the house clutter free

Few chores to do daily

Few weekly chores

A monthly cleaning schedule

Spring cleaning

Keeping the clutter at bay

Conclusion

The Tiny House Lifestyle

Having an immense increase in the popularity, tiny houses have emerged in most parts of the world as people have decided to downsize their lives. The structure of these houses is usually less than 300 feet, it is not necessary that if anyone is moving in a tiny house, they are sacrificing their comfort level. By incorporating thoughtful as well as innovative designs, homeowners have transformed these small areas into a lively place which is full of life and has its connection with not only family and friends but, with nature as well. Deciding to live within such small houses also frees oneself from wastefulness and mortgages, along with the desire to keep up their lifestyle with others.

The recent financial as well as housing collapse (2008-2012) shook most people and left them not only without jobs and retirement plans but, with their homes as well. This economic reality left many people to question their status quo and seek options that are livable, as well as affordable.

Additional benefits associated with the movement to tiny houses include reduced cost of living, yard maintenance, as well as the realization of huge reductions within energy consumption along with home chores with little or no waste. Moreover, it has also managed to attain increased status in resolving the issue of the requirement of emergency shelters or temporary housing.

Over the last 40 years, the size of an average home in the United States increased its size to 1,000 sq. ft. which eventually doubled the living space amount of a person since 1973. However, nearly a decade ago, when the midst of the boom in the housing industry was realized and there was an explosion of constructing luxury and upsize homes within the suburbs of the United States (McMansion), there came into being a smaller and quieter movement which soon gained much attention.

Their main idea was to build quality living areas which will be of lesser square footage but, will include required usage spaces. The concept was named to be 'Not So Big House' and ignited a trend which eventually reflected the economic state of the country. With the struggling housing market today, this idea gained growing conversation and most people decided to shift in tiny houses to reduce as well as reuse.

A typical tiny house can be an average of 100 to 400 square feet and has all the enmities a home requires or that are present in twice as big as that home. These homes can also be as small as 80 square feet or as large as 700 square feet. These homes resemble mostly to studio apartments and can be customized as per the personal tastes and requirements of homeowners.

This concept has crossed all economic boundaries and even multi-millionaires are building off-grid tiny houses not only to show off in the society but, to brag their rights as well for the solutions associated with tiny houses along with dealing the issue of homelessness within the tough economic times.

But before you jump into anything, you should first know the 'basics' of what you're getting into. Here are the preliminary things you should know about tiny home living:

Actual space you have to work with

Knowing the actual space, you have to work with is the first thing you have to know. You cannot rely on estimates as you plan your house. Remember that your space is limited so every area must be planned out completely. No area should be taken for granted or wasted, and to be able to do that you need to know the exact space you've got to work with.

Number of divisions you intend your home to have

After knowing the area you have to work with, the next thing you have to determine the divisions you want your home to have. Would you like your living room to be bigger than your dining and kitchen area? Do you want to have 2 bedrooms fitted in? At this stage of your planning, you'll get to identify your priorities and your plan on executing them. Just make sure that you'll be realistic enough in considering the limited space you have to work with.

Purpose for your move

Knowing the purpose behind your decision could help a lot in the house design department. Do you want a small house for easier mobility? If yes, you can make a house out of light materials and attach some wheels. Do you want a small house because you want a lighter cost of living? Then maybe you should build a house that's easily maintained.

Things you can bringing with you

Having a tiny house requires you to be more thorough in considering the things you'll be taking with you. You cannot bring all your belongings with you especially if there are a lot of them. You have to choose which among them you want to keep and which of them will be left behind.

House theme

The fact that you have a tiny house doesn't mean that your house should be plain and boring. You can still add in some piece of you in there. Do you want a modern-looking house? A simple log cabin? Or a tree house? This issue should be threshed out as early as possible in the planning stage of your house.

Light and ventilation

Every house needs good light and ventilation. This can be a bit challenging to plan in a tiny home. For one, you do not have much room to place a huge window without exposing too much of the inside interior. Moreover, the walls of your small home are one of the things that you could use to maximize the space by putting in it some shelves and hooks. Plan ahead so that this will not be a problem later on.

Building and zoning laws

The fact that you are living small gives you an advantage, but not an exemption from building and zoning laws. Building and zoning laws are stricter when it comes to large houses and buildings, and are more lenient when it comes to small, light houses. To be sure, do a research on these laws to ensure that you will not be violating any.

Durable materials

Knowing what type of materials your house is going to built from should take some planning on your part. If you want to have a log cabin, make sure that you're only using quality logs and the same is true for concretes. Since you are planning on living small, make sure that every inch of your house counts. After all, you'd still be spending fewer on a small house because lesser space would have to be covered.

Number of people to be accommodated

Your house would be you and your family's shelter, so you'd better make sure that it can accommodate everyone. The crucial part in this one is the division of the house.

If, for instance, you have two kids in tow, you have to make sure that there is enough space in your house to accommodate at least 3 bedrooms. You can adjust the divisions if necessary, i.e. make the living room smaller so that you could squish in one more bedroom. The number of people to be accommodated should be laid out at the earliest stage of the planning to avoid alterations later on.

These things could serve as your

personal checklist at the start of the planning. Only upon crossing out each can you really say that you've done your homework well. If you are satisfied that you have done everything stated above, then you can already move on to the next stage.

The idea to live small is gaining popularity and the communities are multiplying. Approximately, 2 out of every 5 tiny homeowners are aged 50 or above. In addition to this, tiny houses are also being used by many people to conduct workshops and host events and most builders as well as designers are catering this demand. Tiny houses offer a new way of thinking about houses and are considered to be an excellent option for the elderly.

Many Americans are spending almost one-third or almost half of their income on their housing schemes. Living in tiny houses take less of paychecks or savings in arranging a roof over their heads. As per a frequently-cited infographic from The Tiny Life, which is a website devoted to provide information about small living, it was recorded that 68% of tiny homeowners are living without any mortgage charges in comparison to 29.3% of other homeowners in the United States.

A standard sized home in US has an average price $272,000 however; this price can reach up to $500,000 if the rate is combined with a 30-year mortgage at the current rate of interest. On the other side, the average cost of a tiny house is $23,000 if it is built by the homeowner. However, this price will increase if built through a builder.

Chapter 2

Benefits of Tiny House Lifestyle

The tiny house movement is supported with a number of factors that an individual face in their daily lives. These are considered to be the most significant issues that are being faced by people living in towns, cities and counties.

People have different reasons why they opt to live in a tiny house. If you are considering making the move, you should first have your reasons in check. Ask yourself "what do I get from living in a tiny house?"

Once you become aware of your

motivations, it will become easier for you to visualize the house you want to have. If you're having a hard time coming up with your reasons, take a look at the following benefits of living small:

Lesser cost

Majority of the people who decide to live in a tiny house is motivated by the promise of lesser expenses. While some are forced by their limited budget, others voluntarily choose to live in small houses for practical reasons, i.e. lower maintenance cost and real estate taxes, more savings for retirement, etc. No matter what angle you decide to look into it, you'll definitely save a ton by living in a smaller space.

Reduced carbon footprint

Small houses produce lesser carbon footprint, use lesser materials, and make lesser impact on the environment. They are a good option for environmentalists, and generally for everyone who cares about preserving the environment.

Low maintenance

Smaller houses are comparably easier to maintain than big houses. For one, the space to cover is smaller, hence easier to clean and repair. You'll need fewer cans of paint of you want to repaint the house, a smaller roof to overhaul the roofing, and lesser water to scrub the floor. More importantly, you'll save on time and effort as you will finish your maintenance quicker than you'll do in a big house.

Bare essentials

The limited space that you have will somehow force you to bring to your house only the 'bare essentials'. Because of this, you will be compelled to bring in only the things you really need and leave the clutter or unnecessary things behind. This will keep your home simpler and mostly clutter-free. You'll also learn how to prioritize your belongings properly. This could also affect how you spend in the future since you will be wiser when it comes to bringing in new things to your limited space.

Personal space for single people

Independence is something that living small can give a person. Since not everyone intends to build their own families in the future, unmarried individuals have found their perfect place in a small house. This is so not because it is less costly, or because it is easily maintained, but because the little space is already enough to fulfill their needs.

Mobility

If you cannot stay put in a place for too long and you're one of those people who want travel to be an everyday affair can surely count on the mobility that a small house can offer. You'd be surprised to see that more and more people are already adopting the small house on wheels fashion nowadays. Small houses provide comfort to travelers as it serves two purposes – a shelter and transportation.

However, you need not put on wheels on

your house just to enjoy mobility. Some people who are steadily going from one place to another due to work and other matters, also find comfort in small houses. Instead of having a big house in one place, others opt to buy two small houses in two places instead. This allows them to have a place to sleep in wherever they might be caught at night.

Be more in control of your life – particularly your finances

Living in a big house could be a standard wish among people, but you don't have to do it if you don't want to. A small house is a good alternative for expensive big house living, reminding you that you always have a choice when it comes to running your life.

More resources

A lesser expense in running a tiny house could only mean one thing – more resources for you! Who says your resources should be depleted on house building and maintenance? There is so much more to life than a house.

For instance, you could use the money you're saving on monthly expense for your travel allowance or tuition fee. You could buy the car you've been saving for, or start the business you've been eyeing for the past 2 years. Living in a tiny house could be one of those big steps that will allow you to channel your resources properly.

A wiser lifestyle

Tiny house living can teach you a lot of things about life and yourself including knowing your priorities, channeling of resources, wiser spending and more. Sooner or later you'll realize that you've becomes wiser that you were before and you are leading a wiser lifestyle centered on practicality, good planning and flawless execution.

Not everyone who wants to live in a small house is forced to do so. As you can see, some people voluntarily made their decision because living in a small house is clearly a good option for many.

Environment and energy

The basic definition of tiny house includes a part that they are built from materials that are not only categorized to be renewable materials but, are environmentally conscious as well. For this purpose, such houses represent an excellent option for cities and towns who are looking for constructing homes that are offering environmentally sustainable options within the housing industry.

As per a survey conducted by TinyHouseBuild.com, a website devoted to provide information related to the building of tiny houses, constructing an average traditional house consumes three quarters of an acre of forest which is equivalent to seven full-logging trucks that are worth of supplies. Contrasting to this situation, construction material of tiny houses are equal to that of a half logging truck.

Another benefit associated with tiny houses are that they save energy consumption as well. An average home in the United States requires 12,733 kilowatts of energy every year to operate and emits about 1,144 pounds of carbon dioxide on an annual basis.

Many tiny houses obtain their utilities, sewage and water supply in a manner through which traditional houses do –

connecting with electrical grids and using other public utilities. However, this can be done only if the city or the particular community allows this for. If not, then tiny house can make solar panel system or standard generators or a combination of both as their source of energy. Water sources can include well or rainwater treatment system which also includes the feature of filtering the water and heats it through a propane water heating system.

As regards the sewage system, there are several options open. Some tiny homeowners prefer composting toilets which make use of the natural way of decomposition as well as evaporation so as to eliminate wastes. Other option includes using incinerator toilets which has a process of burning wastes rather than flushing it away. Also some people may go for septic systems or uses a removal system of a holding tank which is quite similar to what is being used portable toilet providers.

Emergency and conversion housing

Tiny houses have been considered to be a great option in terms of temporary shelter. A great example of this is the 'Katrina Cottages' which were built to find relief from Hurricane Katrina along the Gulf Coast. These cottages were durable, attractive and 300 foot tiny houses which were designed to serve as an alternative of hard-to-obtain and unpopular trailers that were provided by the Federal Emergency Management Agency (FEMA) these cottages not only served as an excellent solution to the crisis but, a desirable choice of a house, in general.

In addition to this, tiny houses can also be used as tiny schools or clinics which can be transported to respective communities in time of need. They also serve as a great option for the transition of military personnel.

Homelessness

In order to combat the issue of homelessness, tiny houses are a viable option through which people can be taken off the streets and provided with a living space of their own thereby, offering them a shelter as well as a measure of self-respect.

An example of Eugene, Oregon, can be quoted here where a community developed Opportunity Village which included 30 tiny houses as shelters for those who need it. Every house is spread over 80 square feet of area. There is a common kitchen, bathrooms and community space. These houses were built through donated materials along with $100,000 in private donations.

The economy and development

Another benefit associated with tiny houses are that they can be built on areas which cannot be zoned for regular homes or buildings. A typical action of municipalities is to tear down the structure of the city, clean up such spaces and the offer tax brackets to developers who in turn reestablish communities. However, such an action results in a socially displaced situation. Perhaps these structures can be used as another way to address the present urban challenges like tiny houses which do not require massive investment.

Although, tiny houses are built to have all the basic amenities of life – electricity, water, heat and a kitchen – however, they lack certain aspects which are luxurious though, but are considered to be standard home appliances by most homeowners like a dishwasher, full-sized stove, refrigerator-freezer as well as a washer and dryer. The reason for not having these appliances is obvious however; the residents of tiny houses can seek the services of local businesses.

Also tiny houses do not have much room for food storage which means that residents are more likely to consume what they had bought recently. This eventually means that they are eating fresh food which is a healthy food as well.

Since, these houses rarely have washers and dryers, local laundry services or Laundromats are being used such an infrastructure holds certain community benefits which includes creating job opportunities (picking and delivering laundry services). The cost of obtaining these services to a typical resident of tiny house will either be the same or lesser than what they will be investing in buying a washer-dryer or paying for water, electricity or gas and detergents.

Zoning law blockades and benefits

Since tiny houses does not have the characteristics to be constructed at any place, they are also free from obtaining building permits and are most often treated by law as a type of recreational vehicles. In many communities, people tend to place tiny houses in the yard or on the grounds of a property which they already own or rent or it is the property of their friend or relative. RV parks and campsite are also great location options for tiny houses.

The founder of Minim Homes, a firm dedicated towards assisting people in building micro homes, built his own tiny house over an area of 210 square foot which rests upon a trailer and had a cost of about $30,000.thistiny house was placed in a vacant lot which they bought in Washington D.C.

However, because of local zoning laws, most tiny homeowners in Washington D.C cannot reside on a plot on a permanent basis. There is a lack of standard zoning relative to such structures which can be a challenge for communities to live in such spaces.

Big benefits of tiny houses

Although, there are various benefits associated with living small however, such a lifestyle may not be suitable for everyone. The first issue that is being faced is that of logistical problems that are usually faced by those who have extensive stuff in their houses. This is especially true for those who have a huge collection of books, large pieces of equipment which may be a part of their job or any hobby that involves maintain big items.

Even though, there are options available for bigger tiny houses and which serves to be suitable for couples and families, not every household experiences this level of togetherness especially when there are other options available.

Arranging a party can be quite challenging in tiny houses. Even daily logistics can be a great challenge even tough other options have been devised. The objective of tiny house residents is to thrive and flourish and for this reason they need to attach more with their surroundings. Consumer options should be a less of an issue and relationships should be more important.

Chapter 3

Financial Aspect of Tiny House Lifestyle

Every time, when this factor arises for tiny homes, one quote is worth mentioning,

'Price of anything can be considered as the amount of life one has decided to exchange for it – Henry David Thoreau'

Initially, the tiny house movement started to be a DIY movement. Those who were dreamers of a tiny house also became the builders of the same. Even though, they had no experience regarding the construction of a home started learning about the finer parts as to how a tiny house can be built. This although, there are various drawbacks associated with building your tiny house by yourself like leaking roofs, mold issues in the basement, etc however, this experience provides the opportunity to determine how these and other issues are fixed when they are troubled. Moreover, this also allows tiny home owners to build in a way which will, if not eliminate, minimizes the risk of any area becoming critical.

From the time of the initial movement, the market for tiny houses grew immensely. Many professional tiny house builders started offering their services to those who would not prefer to build the house at their own. The greatest benefit associated with hiring the services of a professional tiny house builder is that not only you receive the same level of care but, you will benefit from the experience they hold and which are certainly not present with DIY builders.

How Much Will a Tiny House Cost?

Similar to that of traditional and bigger homes, tiny houses also range within their price tag greatly depending of the size, materials, systems as well as the fact that your building the house yourself or hiring the services of a professional builder. Regardless of the fact, that your house is of 300 square feet or 3,000 square feet, your intention to use the house will eventually dictate what type of materials and systems will be installed and what amount you need to and want to spend on them.

A tiny house which is around 150 square feet in area can be estimated to cost around $40,000 giving a rough estimate of $266 per square feet. Although, this cost per square feet is quite high however, this is an estimation of what a tiny house can cost as compared to a big, traditional house. Moreover, the cost of maintenance as well as living in a tiny house is just a fraction of the cost of a big house.

A usual concept of the cost of tiny house is that they can cost between $15,000 to $80,000. Those who have building experience and have great access to various salvaged materials along with a couple of friends who can work out in the building process for free, can make the cost of construction to be around $15k. On the other side, if you are making a professional builder construct your tiny house, then the craftsmanship aspect will come into question which will eventually increase the cost of construction reaching at the point of $80k. As per the survey conducted by The Tiny Life, an average tiny house, which is built by the homeowners themselves along with some friends or hired help, by using salvaged materials as well as some new materials, can cost around $23,000.

How to Save Money on Your Tiny House Construction?

In order to keep the construction of your tiny house within your budget, following mentioned are the top three ways which will help you get the job done.

Build It Yourself

Although, this aspect is quite a difficult one and not every person is willing to take such a task on their hands however, the fact is that handing over the building work to a professional builder will cost you almost double to what you will be spending in a DIY way. If you have access to the right guidance as well as the resources, you will be able to build your own house well. Many people do not have the experience of building a house, however, if you seek guidance from your friends and other professional sources, you will learn in a step by step manner and build your dream home. Moreover, if you build your tiny house by yourself, you will have a sense of achievement which cannot be measured in words.

Select Your Building Materials Well

Finding the right materials at the right price will be very helpful in maintaining your tiny house budget. There are many stores nowadays where you can find excellent deals that will help you keep a check on your budget. The key factor here is that you have access to along with the capacity of incorporating these ideas within your tiny house design. For instance, if you have found some high quality windows at a second retailer, you can buy them and use it in your tiny house building. This and similar other components required to build a tiny house can drastically reduce your cost level.

Be Resourceful/Get Creative

There might be certain instances when you come across building materials that are not only costly but, you can also do nothing about it. In some cases, this can be true however, in most cases, being creative is the key and which will also reduce building costs significantly. For example, panel boards are excellent flooring options and are used by high-end houses however, for most people, installing panel boards can be a fortune. In order to cope up with the situation, the iron-ply material can be used which is a substrate for vinyl floors. Moreover, rather than using the expensive spacing system and panel attachment, you can use the 16d nails so that proper gap is provided as per the designing of every panel.

Although, cutting down costs on building materials is a very good option to maintain your building budget however, it is very important to know where to cut costs and where to spend money. There are some aspects which need to be left alone. For example, the structural elements of a house should never be compromised upon price. In addition to this, you can also spend some money of various finishing aspects like cabinets or appliances. The point is that you have to get your budget inline before starting the building process. Determine what is your budget for every building aspect in your home? Moreover, develop a contingency plan or fund for unforeseen events.

Chapter 4

Organizing: The Basic Principle of Tiny House Lifestyle

If you have a lot of things, you don't need or don't want any more then find a way to get rid of them. Maybe you know someone who can use them. Maybe they can be donated. Maybe you can even sell them and get a little extra money. No matter what you do with them just make sure that you are getting rid of some extra things and that you're getting down to the bedrock of the things that you really want and need to keep and find storage for. This is going to make the process much easier on you.

The most difficult task is to keep the

house maintained at all times. Start with the work slowly and you'll eventually reach your goal! Working slow will keep you motivated as you won't get tired of the workload. And best of all, while you declutter your place, you might find some old important things that might have been displaced! Here you'll get easy DI Y's and creative ideas that will surely inspire you to change the way you feel about arranging these places! It takes some work but it creates a great impression on people who see it, and also makes the house look a lot cleaner and orderly!

After all, do you really need to keep absolutely everything you've owned since you were five? It's time to part with some of those old toys and the broken roller skates. Start paring down your collection a little. You don't need to get rid of everything and you definitely don't need to get rid of the things that are important to you, but it's time to start thinking about some of those old things that you never use.

Decluttering

Living in an untidy house has more disadvantages than you can think of! Want to have a look at some of these troubles that you're sure to be struggling with due to your jumbled up and cluttered house? See for yourself!

- Clutter means many unwanted and old items whose presence might not even be in your knowledge are present in your house. This occupies a lot of space that you could instead use for storing your useful items that get misplaced around the house.

- The more mess you see and feel around you, the more your anxiety grows. All the time, you end up thinking about cleaning up the surroundings and thus there goes your chance to relax!

• The time and stamina you end up wasting in trying to clear up your crowdy surroundings could have instead come to use in some other much better activity.

Once you've gotten rid of some of those things it's time to start looking at the different rooms in your house and how you can use them better than ever. There are definitely some great tips and tricks that you would never have imagined (but they really do work out great).

If every day you spend a hell lot of your precious time to look for things that you misplaced in the house for example your keys, bank cards or your cellphone, it's time to tidy up your house! When you have stacks of books and papers, piles of and piles of stuff that you don't know where to put away, it is then hard to know where to start the cleaning.

So get ready to cut out the clutter

around your house and keep it from coming back with these simple motivations and tricks that will inspire you enough to make you start working right away!

Work small! A house that is strangled in mess isn't easy to clear up. It's necessary to prepare yourself for a while of hard work and then start working small!

- Clear up your drawers, donate the good stuff and if you want, arrange a yard sale to help you get rid of the junk. Try using little containers in your drawers to separate little things like hairpins, paperclips, etc.

- The desks are usually the messiest place in the room, little bits of paper, old receipts and bills, coins and such other junk covers every inch of the desk. Start by making piles on the floor of similar items. For example, a pile of money that you might find on the table, trash, important notes, etc. Recycle all the unnecessary papers and throw away the litter.

• Walk around the house with your laundry basket and grab all those dirty clothes that are lying around! Separate the darks from the lights and toss them in the washer! If you don't have enough space for a dryer, try making a DIY clothesline in your yard. It'll help.

__Planning__

Prior to think about as to how your tiny house will be, it is important to determine as to how things, colors and other elements of a house will be organized. This will require preparing a short list of things that you do in your daily lives. List down all things and chores that you do in everyday life and they occur more often. The list should then be marked on the basis of priority along with those things required to attain the everyday tasks. This will be the line of thought from where the basis of your tiny house will emerge.

From this point onwards, you can sketch floor plans until you come up with something you want to have. You can clear out things by placing masking tapes so as to map out the entire floor. From this plan, you can think about your everyday chores like where to keep the dirty laundry and how much wider the passageways and doors should be so that comfortable passing through them is made possible.

Also at this point you will be able to determine what does not work and needs to be changed. After you have prepared a final and solid plan, keep its aside for a few days so as to allow your mind to come with ideas that your mind cannot think of before. You can also ask your friends to give their feedback about your planning and select the one which you consider to be useful.

On the other side, you can also buy plans in case you do not have any idea or are new to planning a tiny house of your dreams. These plans are available for tiny house owners with respect to their needs as well as budget. This option can also be useful as planning on your own will require a great deal of research. You can also consult various tiny house builders to get your plan finalized. These builders are also capable of providing you with valuable advice which can further enhance the planning process of your tiny house. The final step will be to draft a parts list that will be required to build the tiny house.

Proper Motivation

Inspiration and motivation is really

important before beginning a project. If one is not motivated, the task will become tiring and an inconvenience pretty soon. So once motivated, it's also necessary to stay motivated. You can do this by dedicating a certain period of time to your project everyday instead of piling all the work on yourself all at once. While you're working on the project, do not do any other leisure work or you'll tire yourself quickly and then you'll react aggressively towards your work.

Now as you begin decluttering the house, start with the room which needs very little work as looking at a load of work on your first day might freak you out.

Create a schedule so it doesn't interrupt with your outdoor life. Make a list of your tasks and keep ticking off the work you've done, this will keep you strongly motivated. Don't hesitate in tossing off your old belongings that you don't need anymore. Throw it out or donate it if you want to. Are you ready?

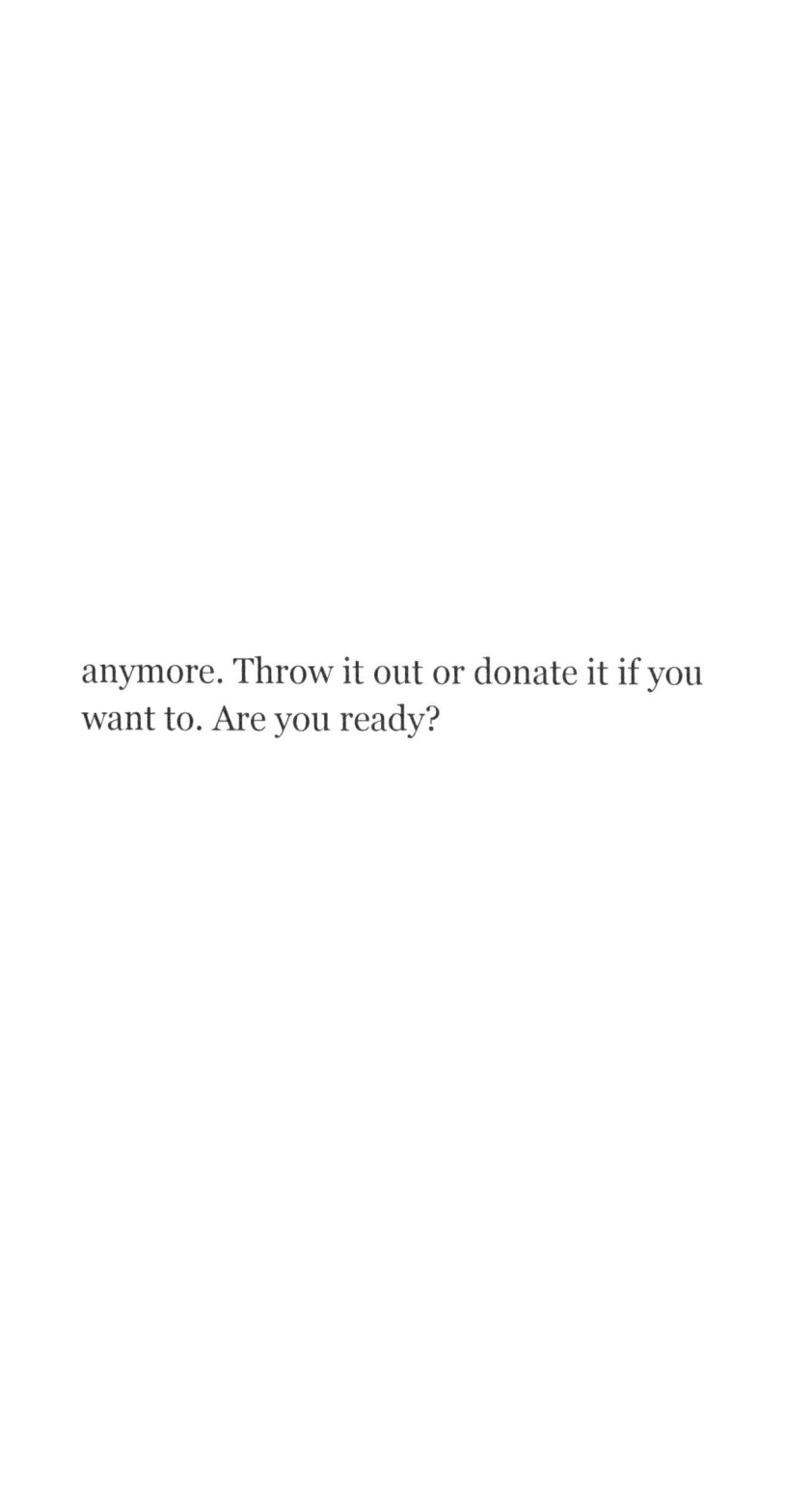

Chapter 5

The Entrance

When guests and visitors come to your place, the first part of the house they see is the door area. That's why, it's better to work your best to organize and keep this place decluttered at all times but it can be really messy as every family member uses that area on daily basis. If this area isn't well-kept, you are surely going to face a mess of muddy shoe prints, sprawled shoes and other things by the end of the day! So why not maintain that area and keep it classy to cast a good impression on unannounced guests?! Here are some tips to help you to declutter the entryway!

- Place an entrance mat near the door so it can absorb the mud and dirt that shoes bring in!

- Use some of your spare time to clean and declutter the entry way on daily basis.

- For wearing shoes, buy a low bench with a built-in cabinet to store all your shoes.

- If you don't have enough space for a cabinet, you also have an option of a 'behind the door organizer'! Use it to store your pet leashes, sunglasses, wallets and other everyday items that get misplaced easily!

- Install hooks on the wall to hold your coats, bags, scarves and umbrellas.

- Keep a trash can or a shredder near the door so that you can get rid of junk mail immediately.

- You could also install a shelf on the wall to hold boxes labeled with each family member's name, this could hold their everyday bills, wallets, sunglasses, etc.

• You could also keep a big vase by the door, not only would this look decorative but you could use them to store your umbrellas!

• Put up mirrors around this area to give an illusion or a larger space.

• Install a key hanger on the wall to hold all your keys!

• A great idea to write down your notes and to place all the new letters and mails, would be to hang up a white board for the notes and reminders with a draw underneath designated for the mails.

Chapter 6

<u>Storage</u>

Just because you have a tiny house doesn't that you can't live large. If you lack closet storage space or you are trying to organize and maximize your small house, the first step is to build. In this chapter, there are projects and tips on how you can create additional storage for your home without compromising the small space you have to work with.

Maximize those Closets

Use all the nooks and crannies of the closets that you have in the house. Invest in a storage system – add in plastic containers, wire racks, shelves, or partitions to keep closets organized. Aside from minimizing the clutter, it makes it easier to find stuff, unlike when things are just kept away in drawers that are not well-organized.

Use Vertical Dividers

There are a lot of benefits to vertical dividers; they save you and/or free you a lot of space to utilize, they are easy to use, and you can even find pull-out types. Vertical dividers make it easier to store casserole trays, cake/baking pans, and serving dishes. They are easy to retrieve, too. If you still have extra slots, you can store cookbooks and/or your favorite food magazines. These are great space savers.

Utilize the Area under the Stairs

The space under the stairs in a tiny house gives you a lot of possibilities. Let your imagination fly and create unique storage areas. You can build in cupboards, drawers, and shelves to keep living room clutter out of the way. If you are into buying print books, you can utilize that space under the stairs and turn it into a book shelf or create a study area where you can have a small table built or put the phone there. Another excellent idea is to build and hide an entire bathroom or a home office.

Your options are endless if you let your imagination fly. You can do just about anything with it.

Create a Mudroom Bench

If you have a tiny house, chances are you don't have a space for a hallway from the main door or even a closet to put away some utility items, umbrellas, or coats/raincoats. If it's raining outside, you can't afford to have messy and rain-soaked raincoats and umbrellas staining your best rug and ruining your hardwood floor. Why not build a stopping area just by the door where you can leave them? You may have flip-top bench storage built- complete with coat hooks and open top shelf. Guests can hang their coats or bags when they come for a visit. This space would be versatile; kids can even play and spend time there.

Stack them Below

Utilize the space under a corner table or

a home office desk. You can put several baskets, small boxes, or bins where you can keep books and other stuff that you don't want lying around the house. Remember the table mentioned under the stairs? You can utilize that space for this purpose as well, so you can get additional storage space.

Go Minimalist with Your Living Room Furniture

Usually, a tiny house doesn't have the defined spaces for a living room provision and the kitchen and dining areas. There may be the separate bedrooms and bathroom but there is an open space for the living room and the kitchen. You can purchase (or custom-build) a smaller set of sofa and center table. Make sure that you have the measurements of the area with you when you go out to shop for home accessories. Have built-in shelves made that will serve as partitions between the kitchen/dining area and the living room area. The less furniture you have, the more organized the area will look.

Less is more. You don't need too many pieces of furniture and decorations because they can use up too much space.

Build Over-door or Over-Window Shelves

Depending on what might work, you can build shelves where you can stash away the clutter from your living room. You may even utilize it as storage for the items that you don't use every day or turn it into an "exhibit" area for the toys that are rarely used by your kids. These shelves may hold baskets or other essential items like plates and bowls that are only used on special occasions.

Add Zen to a Work Den

There are smaller homes that still feature a den, an attic, or spare rooms. Any of these three can be converted into a home office or a small study. To maximize the space, you can build vertical shelves. Monochromatic-themed rooms look elegant, clean, and clutter-free. The room can have a calming effect so that it is easier and lighter to work.

Versatile Ottoman Chairs

The Ottoman brand became popular because of their products' innovative and practical designs. An ottoman chair can serve a lot of purposes – it can provide extra seating, a coffee table, or a foot rest. The company has also come up with newer designs besides the basic round or square types. New versions that have under-lid storage can serve as storage for blankets and or books.

You can also have the upholstery customized to fit your home décor. The storage chairs come with varying height and style that will complement your existing furniture. Their units are stain resistant so if you have pets and small children, this is an ideal choice.

Chapter 7

Living Room

In the living room you may actually be surprised how much space you actually have and how well you can use it as well. That's because your living room is generally one of the biggest in your entire house. You probably have some space that you don't even think about because it's in an odd location or it's just a little bit small.

Small spaces are great for adding storage because they really have no other purpose. You have nothing else that you can do with them and so you might as well put a small table in or a toy box for your children. It also frees up some of the more obvious space that you really don't want to use this way.

The living room is the main station of family gatherings, it's where many tasks take place during the day and that's why it really is the most difficult place to maintain and keep clean. When you're expecting guests, this is the first room they see and that's why it should be elegant, beautiful and always spotless! The trick of keeping this room tidy is to set ground rules for your family. The kids need to know that whatever they use, needs to be kept back in it's place. Every family member should take a part in keeping the room absolutely maintained and uncluttered at all times. Some key points to keep in mind while furnishing and keeping the living room are listed below!

- Using cabinets with French doors gives an elegant and classy look to the room.

- Instead of a small TV trolley, invest in a large TV cabinet with storage cubes to hold your things.

- If you want to keep things on shelves, then first set them inside pretty boxes so it that the shelves do not look messy.

- Little decorative baskets and bins would be a great idea to store toys and games.

- A coffee table with built-in space for storage would be great to hold books, magazines and tissues.

- Stack video cassettes and DVDs in boxes and keep them in the TV cabinet.

- To avoid losing the remote controls again and again, designate a box for them on a head-level shelf.

- Custom made bins to fit the size of the empty space beneath your coffee table can be used for storing many different items!

- Conceal shabby equipment's and other devices in baskets and put them away in the cabinets.

- Invest in a trash bin with a lid. This will reduce all the trash lying around the room after a long day!

- Try to keep the floor spotless by placing all the bins and baskets in the cabinet when not in use.

- Use a tall trash bin to hold fireplace tools.

Choose sofas on raised legs

Sofas on raised legs create the impression of more space because it allows you to see the space between the seat and the floor. More often than not, these types of sofa are also less bulky than floor-length ones.

Put on mirrors that will reflect the view outside

The living room is more likely the first place to set foot in once your past the main door. As it is, it must have a great access to the outside view though the door and windows. Take advantage of this view by putting a mirror that reflects the view outside. This will make your living room look more spacious and welcoming. The bigger the mirror, the better!

Keep things minimal

The living room is the place you will accommodate your guests, hence it must be comfortable enough to serve its purpose. Keeping things simple in the living room serves two purposes: first, it makes the space look wider because the attention will remain fixed at the focal point, whether it's the sofa or the large drapery; and second, it makes the ambience more relaxing.

Avoid bulky chairs

There is really no room for bulky anywhere in your tiny home, most especially in the living room! Get rid of those bulky chairs and replace them with lean, but equally functional chairs.

Do not go too big on paintings

In a tiny space, the rule of thumb is that you have to establish a focal point. The focal point will dictate how your space would look like as it catches the attention of your guests. In the living room, a good focal point would be the sofa. If you choose the sofa as your focal point, make sure that the sofa will look perfect in your little space, not too crowded or bulky.

Have foldable seats instead of bean bags

While bean bags can make a comfortable seat, it can consume much of your living room space. Trade these bean bags for foldable chairs that you can tuck away when not in use. With foldable chairs, you wouldn't have to worry about extra seats anymore!

Board-less sofas

Board-less or backless sofas can provide additional seat without occupying much of your space. In fact, backless sofas can be placed in the center of your living room without looking out of place.

Add a piece or two of small indoor plants

Give some natural ambience to your living room by adding a piece or two of small indoor plants. Small indoor plants are effortlessly stylish and they would go well with any type of furniture.

Choose chair/sofas will small arms

There is nothing wrong with choosing a sofa or chair with an arm. In fact, the arm adds comfort to it. However, make sure that you choose ones with small arms. This will provide comfort without making the sofa or chair too bulky.

Go for a wall-mounted flat screen TV

Your living room entertainment set should not cost you too much space. Try having your flat screen TV wall mounted to save a little space in the room. More than saving space, wall mounted TVs look so much cooler!

Shelves

Shelves are a great place to display some of the things that you own (like little knick-knacks or pictures) without taking up a lot of table space. You don't have to sort through quite as many of those knick-knacks that you love to try and get rid of them. You'll have space on the walls to display them and you can change them out whenever you want. It doesn't really hide anything, but it does make it much easier to enjoy your space without worrying too much about the clutter.

The Bookshelf

If you're a book lover like me, I am so

sure you have about a hundred books stacked in many places around the house. It can be difficult to find the one you want to read when don't have a designated place for them because then they can be anywhere in the house!

How about making some amendments in your book collection? I understand the feeling of wanting to keep every single book with you, but it's necessary to sort them out! Let's start with helping you figure out what you want to keep and what you want to donate!

- Take out all the books that are currently stuffed in your bookshelf.
- Donate or sell old books that you've already read.
- Make piles of books that fall in the same category.
- Stack them on the bookshelves according to their genre.

If you have now a small pile of books left over, get rid of your huge cabinet and replace it with a small shelf. Now let this shelf hold a limited amount of books by donating the ones you read and buy new books only if you really want to read them. You could also buy books in the eBook form to save space on the shelves.

Wall Cabinet

In this room especially you may find a wall cabinet a great blessing in disguise. These can be used to hide away your TV or to store more of your items like movies, video games or even CD's. You have the ability to hide them away easily by putting your wall cabinet somewhere that anyone can admire the way it looks but no one is easily going to see inside. On the other hand, if you want them to be able to see your items you can put glass doors on the front to let everyone know what you have. (If you're able to stay organized this can be a nice way to display your movie collection.)

Ottoman

If you don't have an ottoman couch you should definitely get one. After all, an ottoman is great for storing plenty of things from your magazines and mail to blankets, remotes, controllers or anything else you use in the living room but don't necessarily want to leave sitting out for your guests to see. It's all hidden away in something that's also beautiful and perfect for sitting on.

Toy Chest

Tired of all those toys laying around your floor when the kids don't pick them up? Or maybe they are just piled in a corner of your room cluttering up space. Well none of those are good options and they're easily remedied. Instead of leaving the toys out all the time put a small toy chest in a corner of your living room. Make sure all of the toys get put away in the chest each night before your children go to bed. It's going to make your space look a lot neater than before and it's also going to help you have more floor space in the long run.

Chapter 8

<u>Kitchen</u>

Your kitchen is the perfect place to store your dishes, silverware, appliances and other utensils but it can often seem like you just don't have enough space for everything that you need. So what do you do? Well there are plenty of areas that you've probably never considered for putting all of your extra items. Some of them are outside of the kitchen (like the dining room options we'll talk about next) and others are right there in the kitchen but in spaces that you probably didn't think about previously.

When you host a dinner party or when guests come to your place, they always enter the kitchen and would a messy kitchen make a good first impression? No! So that's why you should take all possible steps to keep your kitchen classy and spotless at all times! Let's have a look at some different parts of a basic kitchen and their organization techniques.

Smart Kitchen Storage

Open storage shelves are more appealing than regular kitchen cupboards. If you want to separate the kitchen from the dining area but still have an open and airy space, this is a great idea. A small wall divider with floor-to-ceiling shelve partitions can turn a small kitchen area into two separate rooms. These open shelves are perfect for storing and showcasing your favorite glassware and china pieces.

Don't Compromise an Open Floor Plan

Instead of a divider with floor-to-ceiling shelf partition, you may opt for a half-wall divider to separate a small kitchen from the dining area. This doesn't eat up the area and instead gives the illusion of a larger, combined space. This may also serve as a built-in storage and an occasional bar.

Do not compromise the area's open floor plan because you can make any area functional with more elbow room if you use the right accessories and build appropriate fixtures.

Keep Trash Out of Sight

If your space still allows, you can build a pullout system for your trash can in the kitchen. Utilize the space below the sink and build a pullout drawer.

Build an Island

If your kitchen has enough space for an island, then you can have one built. It can give you additional work space and an extra place to eat. If you live alone, you can eat here and do away with buying a dining table. If you have occasional visitors, you can purchase collapsible tables and chairs so you can just take them out each time you have company.

You can build drawers and cabinets under the island for additional storage.

Utilize the Corners

The corner spaces are often neglected and left unused. Think of a lazy Susan type of cabinet design where you can keep baking dishes or pans and pots. You can make it uncomplicated and just build corner drawers for additional storage spaces for kitchen supplies, making them easily accessible.

How about a built-in storage cabinets and drawers? You can use upper compartments for displaying kitchen accessories or the drawers can house your microwave and over. The cabinets at the bottom allow you to further de-clutter your countertops.

Have a dilemma because of small kitchen area? Rethink your kitchen design. It doesn't have to be placed in a traditional position. The corner space and build a sink and add in a countertop that can double as food prep area and dining area.

If you have plans for the sink, then utilize the corner for your stove and add a shelf on top so you can use it as storage for cooking items.

The Cabinets

All of your kitchen accessories and supplies should be stored in cabinets to avoid visual clutter around the place. Kitchen islands with built-in dining table or cabinets are a great option for small kitchens.

- Use the cabinets in your kitchen island to store kitchen supplies such as napkins, paper towels, etc.
- If you have a large nook in your kitchen, build a small banquette for family dinners.

- Install spotlights under your kitchen cupboards, this will provide light on your kitchen counters and will give an elegant look to your kitchen!

- Hide all the kitchen appliances! They do not look very appealing on the counters and putting them away will save a lot of space!

- Install a pretty wall shelf to hold your cookbooks, this will give a classy look to your kitchen.

- Hang hooks behind the kitchen door to hold your aprons and pot holders.

- In the shelf which is easily accessible, store all the pots and dishware that you use frequently.

- You can keep all your pot lids in a magazine rack so you won't have to worry about how you would stack different shaped pots on each other!

- Use a CD rack to hold your plates.

- Hang up a shoe organizer in your cabinet under the sink to hold all your cleaning products and you could also use lazy Susans for this.

- Appoint cabinets for different dishware. For example, a cabinet for bake ware, dinner plates, cookware, etc.

- Slide out cabinet drawers can have place for a cutting board on top.

- Keep the kitchen utensils you use the most in your top most drawer.

- Small things that you need on the counter can be kept on lazy Susan's so that they occupy less space.

- You could install a hanging pot rack above your kitchen island to save space in your cabinets. This will also give an organized look to your kitchen.

- Pretty utensils can be kept in vases on the counter top for decoration purposes.

- Use a magnetic strip on your kitchen wall to hold all your knives and cutlery, this will save a lot of space in your drawers.

- Slide out kitchen islands can save a lot of space!

- You could also install hooks on the wall above your counter to hold your tea cups.

- Use a funky cake stand to hold your cleaning utensils on the sink!

The Pantry

Is your pantry overflowing with open boxes, cans of expired products and overstocked groceries? Then it's time you clear it up and organize your pantry! Here are some inspiring ideas to get you working on your pantry makeover! Not only will uncluttering the pantry save you a lot of money, but it will also help you save time as you won't have to rummage around the shelves.

- Make a point of using up every inch of space by buying jars and baskets of sizes that would fit your pantry well.

- Gather all the things on the country and sort them.

- Throw away the expired products and gather all the open boxes into one.

- Place all the soda cans, food cans, food in plastic bags and other such things in separate baskets.

- Label all your containers and baskets.

- Use lazy Susans to store spice bottles, cake decorations, food colors or other bottled products for easy view.

- Use a hanging organizer on your pantry door to hold packs that are already opened.

- Stack larger items on the pantry shelves.

- Use a wine rack to hold your spice bottles.

- Use airtight containers and boxes to hold macaronis and other items.

- Use paperclips to seal open packages.

- Store foods that you eat often on shelves that are on eye-level.

- You could also use buckets to hold drinks and beers.

- Maximize your space by adding extra shelves and drawers.

- Regularly clean your pantry to keep it maintained!

The Fridge

This is another place which is frequently used by the family members during the day. It can be quite difficult to maintain a fridge which can get very messy at times! Such as spills, expired products, overstock, etc. To organize a fridge, you could use some of these 'tested and loved it' ideas!

- Firstly, use a magnetic grocery list on the door of the fridge. This way, when someone notice's that an item has finished, they can write it down on the note, making it easier to know what to get from the grocery store.

- You could also use magnetic spice holders so they can be attached to the fridge.

- Use baskets to store your grocery in the fridge, its easier as you can slide them out easily.

- Keep the leftovers, drinks and ready-to-eat food on the top shelf and keep the raw to-cook items on the shelves below.

- Keep the fruits and vegetables in the drawers so they stay fresh.

- Place a small open bowl of baking soda anywhere in your fridge, this chases away the foul odor and you just have to change it every six months.

- Use lazy Susans in your fridge to keep all your spices and little bottles within reach easily.

- If you're using containers, make sure they're see through so you don't have to open them again and again to see what's inside.

- Spread a cling wrap over the shelves so that if something spills, you can just rip it off and toss It away! Though if you want to get more creative, you could buy some fridge coasters!

Now that your kitchen is organized, wouldn't you like to spice things up with some classy decorations? Here are some ideas that you'll love!

- Keep your fruits to display in large glass jars that come with lids.
- Hang up some pretty frames of inspiring quotes or kitchen wall arts.
- Hang up a framed blackboard so you can note down the shopping list there.
- Show off your pretty china on top of your kitchen cabinets.
- Magnetized containers on your fridge can hold many useful supplies that you use regularly!

Wall Hanging Pot Rack

Hang your pots and pans up on the walls instead of using up some of your valuable cabinet and cupboard space. You may actually be surprised how great they look hanging up and you will be able to put different items in the spaces that you would otherwise have to reserve for your pots. Plus, they're actually going to be a lot more convenient when you're looking to use them for your next meal.

Utensil Rack

Look for a utensil rack that either hangs on your wall or will sit on top of your cupboards as well. This takes them out of your drawers and you'll have even more space for things that can't be hung up easily. You will want to use these racks for larger utensils like serving spoons or large knives. Make sure everything that's sharp is out of the reach of your children. You don't want them to get hurt because the knives are no longer stored safely away in a drawer.

Baskets

Do you have some extra space at the top of your cupboards? A lot of people do. And that space is usually considered dead space. If you use little baskets to put all of your smaller things, however, you'll actually be able to use that space and still get to the items that are stored there. You also won't have to worry about it looking bad because the baskets will look cute up on the shelf. If you need to store a lot just look at getting larger baskets (but fewer of them) to make it appear less cluttered. You can store anything you want up here because most likely no one will see any of it.

Boxes

If you really need more space think about all the dead space inside your cabinets. Most of your stuff is probably pretty flat right? Or it doesn't come all the way to the front of the door? If this is the case, then you have a lot of empty air that you could be using. Install wire boxes to the inside of your cabinet doors. You'll be able to fill them with different types of items like wax paper or spices, and then you can use up some of the excess space.

Toe Kick

Have you ever heard of a toe kick? If you haven't then you shouldn't feel upset. It's actually a relatively small number of people who ever have. What this is really is a small drawer located all the way at the bottom of your cabinet, where the base is. In most cabinets this is dead space underneath the drawer or door where it meets the floor. In some however, there is another drawer under here that is thin but long, allowing it to hold more of your pots and pans if you aren't able to store them otherwise.

Add Levels

Instead of just putting everything on the few shelves that you have in your cupboards try to build up as well. You'll probably be surprised to notice that you have plenty of space above your current items. A lot of stores sell shelves that you can easily install over the current shelves so that you have a little extra space. Feel free to put anything in this space and definitely make the most of it. There's more up there than you may have expected.

Chapter 9

__Dining Room__

The dining room is probably not a place that you think of putting a lot of storage. After all, it's the place where your table goes right? Most people don't think about putting a lot of storage in this area but that doesn't mean you can't. It's actually an extension of your kitchen as well. You can store a lot of the leftover kitchen items that you really need but don't have space for in your dining room and you'll be able to make room without having to store your leftover things in the basement or attic.

Opt for glass tables

Glass tables are not only beautiful; they also make your area look more spacious because of the transparency. The transparency of glass allows views from all sides of the room. Despite its dominance in the area, it doesn't crowd the view of the dining room.

Allot moving space for chairs from the dining table

Comfortable movement should always be a priority, especially in the dining room where people move around to serve food and eat. Make sure that you allot enough moving space for chairs in the dining table in case the people have to go around and sit again.

The same is true with the moving space

in the table. Make sure that people are not in bumping distance with one another as they eat.

Avoid chairs with tall/huge backrests

Backrests can provide much comfort, but you must be careful in choosing them especially if your space is limited. Avoid chairs with very tall or wide backrests that clog the space.

Go for tables with a detachable leaf

A lot of tables available in the market today come with a detachable leaf. Get one of those tables. These tables will provide you a backup in case you need more table space and a way out in case you need space in the dining room.

Consider getting a round table

Round tables are more flexible because it doesn't have corners that would hinder the guests from moving freely. This will allow the guests to feel more comfortable even in a small setup.

Armless dining chairs

The dining area is one of the areas in the house that is used for a particular purpose, which is dining. By its very nature, the dining room is one which is used for a limited time only. The more important feature of the dining room is its effectiveness in giving the guests a good dining experience.

Since comfort for a long period of time is out of the picture, you can definitely place on armless dining chairs to make the area look more open and spacious.

The dining rooms are two of the most important areas in any home. It is crucial that you design them taking into account their purpose and of course, the space you have to work with. Just follow the tips above and you'll find it an easier job!

China Cabinet/Hutch

If you have a lot of dishes or kitchen utensils, you can use a china cabinet or hutch to store some of the excess that you don't use every day. These don't have to have glass doors on them even though you've probably usually seen these the most often. You can get ones that have plain doors which are solid and hide away anything you don't necessarily want others to see. This means you don't just have to use them to store your best china. You're actually able to use them for some of your older dishes or some of the small appliances that you probably don't use all that often. Plus, you'll be making the most out of space that you probably don't use any other way.

Pantry

Do you have a rather large dining room but not a very large kitchen? If you do, then you can actually consider adding in an extra pantry in the dining room. This will cut down on the amount of space available in your dining room which is why you want to consider the entire family before you try to remove any space. Make sure there's going to be enough room. If there is, you can create a walk-in pantry that will allow you more space to store food as well as kitchen utensils.

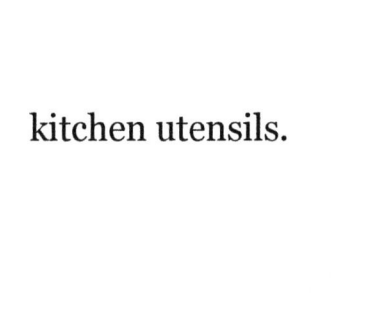

Chapter 10

<u>Bedroom</u>

Basically, your bedroom is the place where you store all your personal things. You might face storage problems in a small bedroom but a creative mind would love the idea of using every nook and cranny of the little room! The solution to the lack of space for storage is to use multifunctional furniture in your house, especially in your bedroom. If you're new to the house, take measurements of every nook in your room and hit the furniture market! Some of the ideas for your furniture are listed below.

- Use wall shelves in your bedroom, you can store every kind of item you want in pretty boxes.

- Use foldable desks wherever possible!

- Wall beds or sofa beds are also an option you could look up to.

- Storage cubes (stackable) can be used to store a variety of items!

- Full length stand mirrors with built-in space for your jewelery has it's advantages.

- Foldable stools can be of great benefits not only in your bedroom but also in the kids room!

- Beds with drawers underneath them.

- Cabinets above the bed can be used to store extra blankets and pillows.

Sometimes the bedroom can be the most

cluttered and disorganized areas of the home since no visitor would go inside or take a peek of what's in there. People often put away stuff in there and when you keep doing that, soon the bedroom will be full of things that do not even belong there.

Your bedroom can be cleaned up and organized step by step. Remember, working steadily will keep you motivated so do not rush into things and try to declutter the room all at once resulting in a very depressed and tired you. Let's start the first step.

Cleaning up your closet

No matter how much we try to keep our closet neat, it always manages to get messy! But don't worry, creativity and a little work will help you get rid of the stress you have to face every day searching around for your clothes! Let's begin with..

- Toss out the clothes that are torn or worn out.

- Donate the clothes that you don't like anymore to charity.

- Fold extra sweatshirts and jeans (if you don't have space to hang everything).

- Start with hanging all of your clothes up. Trust me, it's easier to spot your favorite shirt when it's hanged rather than rummaging around in a pile of folded clothes.

- Place your undergarments and socks neatly in separate containers.

- Use the bottom shelf to lineup your shoes, stack your extra stuff such as bath supplies, rags or blankets on the top shelves.

- Take out that large box of photographs! Why stack them in your cupboard when you could easily digitize them and store them in a hard drive?

- Use hooks on the doors of your closet so that you can hang your scarves there.

- Stack away out of season clothes in any place around the house.

- Use shower rings on a hanger to hold your variety of scarves and ties.

- Use containers to store undergarments and socks.

- If your closet is too small, bring the backside of it's door to use by installing a rod.

The bedroom could be one of the most challenging areas to decorate in a tiny house. It should be tight enough to fit yet large enough to accommodate the personal belongings and offer comfort to the person staying in it. To help you out in this task, here are some bedroom decorating tips you could apply:

Do not put in beds that are too large

The bed that you'll buy should be enough to accommodate 2 persons at most. If you put in beds that are too large, it will take up too much space – which you do not have plenty of. If you have to accommodate many, at least opt for pull out or double deck beds. It is best if you make the bed the focal point of the bedroom so that it will look more organized and relaxing. If you want to put a window, make sure that you place it in front of the bed so that it docsn't compete for attention.

Keep the room as open as possible

Avoid putting on bed nets, curtains, or chandeliers in your bedroom. While these accessories add to the style, it only looks good in spacious areas. If you put these items in your bedroom, it will only make the room look claustrophobic. Keep the space as open as possible to make the room appear larger.

In addition to this, make sure that you choose a bed with see through boards i.e. iron bar boards instead of solid woods. This will add to the illusion that the room is larger than it is.

Go for bold designs

With a small bedroom, you have no time for subtlety. Go for either dark or light hues, ranging from chocolate brown to red to sunshine yellow. Whatever effect you're looking for, go for it straight and all out. After all, decorating a small bedroom should not push your budget too much.

Maximize every inch of space

Assess your space and look for possible storage areas i.e. under the bed, ottoman in the window, etc. You can make use of these areas instead of using a large closet for your belongings. You can put shelves in the wall, drawers under the bed and hooks in the door.

Put on artworks

Having a small bedroom doesn't mean that it has to be plain and boring. Put a piece of you in there by placing artworks of your style. For small bedrooms, the most recommended art pieces are paintings. Paintings can accentuate your room without overcrowding it. You can also put on decorative lamps, nice bed fabrics, and colorful carpets.

Do away with the conventional

Having a small bedroom limits you when it comes to space, and it being so, you have every right to veer away from the conventional. Feel free to experiment with décors and furniture arrangement all you want until you discover what best works for you.

Try to get ideas from the internet

You need not rack your brain for bedroom designs before you can get one! Keep in mind that you're not the first one to ever design a small bedroom. There are others who already did what you're doing right now, and there is always the good old internet if you can't find someone to help you out. You can either copy ideas or vary them according to your tastes.

Add a multifunctional bedside table

Who says your bedside table should only hold you lamp? Choose a bedside table that has drawers and shelves in it so you could use it for storage as well. You can even do away with the lamp and instead put the lights in the ceiling for more space.

Add a touch of your own style

Your bedroom, no matter how small, should reflect who you are as a person. You can paint the ceilings and walls in your favorite colors. Just add a touch of your own style in your bedroom such as pictures, paintings and anything that describes you.

There are a whole lot more decorating

ideas that you can learn in the process of decorating your bedroom, so never stop learning!

You can use storage cubes and dividers in your closet to hold your shoes, bags, etc. Little baskets can hold towels and you can store your hats in containers.

Some other ideas for storing things around your bedroom are

- Use the space underneath your bed by placing proper sized plastic pull-out containers there. Here you can store all types of junk you have!

- Install shelves on the bedroom walls. You will be able to store everyday items in pretty boxes on these shelves!

- Use that awkward nook in your room for your relaxation by setting up a reading spot there.

- You could also keep a horizontal set of storage cubes under your bed.

- Use 'over the door' hooks to hang up outfits for the next morning!

- Use boxes in bedside drawers as dividers to keep the clutter from gathering on top of the table.

Don't Forget the Drawers

It is important that every piece of bedroom fixture has drawers or some kind of storage space. When you shop for furniture, choose functional items over adorable ones. Buy a nightstand with drawers. Look not for chunky and chic beds but instead look for units with drawers. You may also have your bed custom built so you can incorporate additional storage.

Consider a Day Bed

If you are one of those people who works from home and work in the bedroom because there is no extra room for office space, purchase day bed instead of a big bed that can take the entire bedroom space.

You may purchase a small table (with drawers, of course) instead of a nightstand so you can use it for your laptop. Choose one that you can use comfortably while you sit on your day bed (or sofa bed).

Maximize the Wall Space

If your room is enough for a bed and a dresser only, maximize the wall space with "floating" shelves and cabinets. Most small apartments or houses have built-in closets for the bedrooms so you can apply the tips mentioned in the first chapter so you can have enough storage space for your closet.

If you want to put in a few decorations, you may hang a fancy mirror and decorative hooks that you can also use to hang bags and coats.

If you need to display a few items on the open shelves, take out only the ones that you use often and keep the others neatly in boxes and trays that you can place under.

You may not even have to get a table for your laptop or computer because you can have a floating computer table built on the wall. You can use the space under to organize boxes and trays for your trinkets and other office items. This is ideal for people who work from home.

Hide Items that are Rarely Used

The spaces under the beds and sofas are great storage areas. If you choose beds with drawers, you can keep the linens and beddings there. They are also ideal to keep away your kids' toys. If you don't have built-in drawers underneath, you can purchase plastic storage boxes with covers so it is easier to see what's inside without the need to open each box.

Set Up a Home Office in Your Closet

Yes, you read it right—it is recommended that you set up your home office inside a closet because this can give you a lot of storage space. You can have built-in shelves there to keep your laptop and office items. When the closet door is closed, you still create a seating space.

Make Every Furniture and Accessory Piece Count

When you have a small house, and this tip can be applied for all the other areas, choose furnishings and decorative items that are multi-functional. Do not buy items that will only take square footage space without actually doing anything for you. Choose a sofa bed, or use two smaller round center tables instead of a big coffee table that take up too much space, or choose side tables and nightstands with functional drawers.

You can still do a lot of things with your tiny house. All you need to do is to keep your imagination and creativity going and you will never go wrong.

Organizing the Kids Room

Tired of begging your children to clean their room? Sick of finding piles of toys tucker under the bed? Maybe you should smooth the clutter and help your kids tidy up the place. It's important to bring your kids to order and teach them how the cleaning is done! Try these projects and ideas to straighten out and craft up the room.

Use Bunk Beds for the Kids' Room

If you don't have extra rooms in the house, rely on the classic bunk beds – they don't take up too much space and they keep an open floor area where the kids can play.

- Don't pressure them into throwing away things that you might think are worthless, start by examining the room with your child's point of view.

- Use furniture that your child can use easily

- When organizing their closet, lower the rod of hanging clothes so they're in the child's reach. You could also fold the clothes and keep them in their dresser.

- Stack away worn out clothes or clothes that are too large for the child.

- Use open baskets in the dresser to keep the socks and undergarments separate.

- Use a big trunk to hold their toys in for easy access.

- It's better to use toy trunks with wheels so it's easy for children to drag it around.

- Hive away some of the toys and bring them later some time so that they look new and interesting to the kids.

- The best kind of bed for a kid's room is the one which has a lot of built-in drawers. This can store a load of little items.

- Small stuff toys can be stored in hanging shoe organizers.

- You could install a magnetic strip on the wall to hold the kid's metal toys such as cars, airplanes, etc.

- If you have a bed without drawers, use the space underneath it! Keep pull-out containers to store things in there.

- Small play items like puzzle pieces should be stored in Ziploc bags.

- Stack up storage bins in one corner of the room and hide them with curtains.

- A small dresser can be kept beside the bed so your child can store bedtime books or novels there for easy reach at night.

- You can creatively store your child's craft supplies in buckets hanging on the wall.

- Create a study zone and a play zone. Things belonging to their zones should be store there so that the room doesn't jumble up.

- Use the backside of the room's door to store stationary, art supplies, etc.

After you've organized the kid's room, it can be hard to keep it maintained. Some of these ways can help you keep your children stay obedient.

- Usually moms say 'time out' doesn't work for them. Maybe so, but here is a good news! You can try by making them do a chore and the time out doesn't finish until the chore is done. No child likes to do chores and thus this will bring an end to their rowdy behavior.

- Warn your kids that if they do not finish a chore (homework, cleaning the room, etc.) on time, they will have to face consequences.

- If they do something mischievous, make them sleep early that night.

- Things that your children leave lying around, keep them in a different place. When they ask you where the item is, tell them they will have to find them. This will eventually bring an end to their 'forgot to put back' habit!

Chapter 11

Bathroom

Having a small bathroom can be difficult at times, but what about when it's messy as well? Tangled up wires of hair appliances and other machines, counter littered with bottle of lotions, hairsprays and God knows what not! Oh yes, that can be a HEADACHE!

In your bathroom you probably use your sink and your closet to store things right? You try to keep everything entirely out of sight so that it looks nicer when guests come over. But you actually don't need to do that at all if you're careful about how you display things.

Here you can refer to some of the best

DIY projects to help you with tidying up your messy bathroom!

- Buy some spice racks from any dollar store and hang them up on your bathroom walls, these can store your little bottles of lotions creams.

- Hook up different sized PVCs on the door of your bathroom cabinet. The bigger ones can hold your hair irons and dryers, and the small ones can hold their folded wires.

- You could also install a file box on the counter to hold appliances.

- Use containers and baskets in your medicine cabinets, name these bins with the name of each family members so it can contain their bathroom supplies.

- You could also use lazy Susans in your cabinet to keep all your cleaning supplies on. This way you can see all of them without having to move them around and create a mess!

- You don't really need a toilet paper holder, you can keep rolls of them on your toilet seat as well!

- Put up a hanging basket near the tub and store all your shampoos and conditioners in there, just like a shower caddy.

- Hang up a shelf on your bathroom wall to store extra supplies such as towels, etc.

- Magnetize your toothbrushes and install a magnetic strip on your bathroom wall. Trust me, that saves a lot of spaces and cuts away a lot of mess too!

- Also, you could use a cake stand on your counter to hold your everyday creams there.

- As you can see, I am too obsessed with using the backside of the doors! So here again I would suggest to use an organizer behind the door to hold many bathroom supplies!

• A few drops of essential oil inside the toilet paper and your bathroom won't stink for a lot of days!

• You can install a wall shelf above the bathroom door and stack extra towels, tissue rolls and other washroom supplies there.

• A wine rack on the bathroom wall can be used to stack rolls of towels!

• A magnetic strip in the medicine cabinet can be used to hang nail clippers, filers, razors, etc.

• Stick hooks behind the bathroom door to hold your robes.

Use Pastel Colors

Refrain from using strong colored-paint. Instead, use pastel colors because they give an illusion of a bigger space. You can use strong colors for bathroom accessories, decorations, and towels.

Use a Glass Door

Ditch the shower curtain and use clear glass door instead. It opens up the shower area so it becomes a part of the whole bathroom. This trick makes the room appear bigger.

Use Indirect Lighting

If there is no natural light coming in the bathroom, you may use recessed lighting. This type of lighting is unobtrusive. You can position it anywhere you prefer and have it focused on any task area.

Provide Natural Light to the Bathroom

If you can have a window installed, it is the best way to let natural light enter the area. You can use window treatments that can be partially opened. You may add in curtains so you can just easily roll the up.

Tubular skylights are also a good alternative to let the sun inside the room.

Maximize the Wall Space

One of the challenges of smaller spaces is having limited floor square footage. The ideal solution is to maximize the wall space. Install "floating" toilet fixtures and "floating" cabinets and drawers. Choose a unique material like bamboo for the door and/or cabinets. Use ocean blue colored tiles to open up the space a little. Stylized lighting can also do the trick.

Space Savers

Recessed shelving is a popular style for small bathrooms; since it gives you wall storage without infringing the square footage of the room. If you have open shelves, arrange the items neatly to avoid looking cluttered.

If you can't use recessed shelving, you may purchase an open shelf metal rack where you can place the toiletries and other bathroom items.

Do you have the standard horizontal shelving below your window? This is an ideal space to use to ensure that your compact bathroom doesn't look cluttered.

Baskets

Get an over the toilet rack and use it to store baskets with some of your stuff in them. These baskets should have nice things like extra soap and shampoo, maybe some hair accessories or some nail polish. You want the things in them to be things you don't mind your guests looking at when they walk into the bathroom.

Laundry Hamper

If you're trying to hide your laundry in the closet you're taking up space that could be used for something else. Instead, get a cute laundry hamper with a lid on it. You won't mind people seeing the hamper and you'll have more space in the bathroom closet for shelves which can hold things like towels and more linens if you have them. The laundry hamper will hold all of your dirty clothes so you don't even have to worry about them.

Large Sink

Get a large sink that has a built in cabinet with it. This is going to give you more space to hide away some of the things that you generally need in your bathroom like a toothbrush and toothpaste. It may also allow you to put some of your towels and washcloths under the sink which could free up your closet for things like linens or bath toys for your children. You want to make the most out all of your space and that's much easier if you start moving things around and looking for the best way to store them.

Chapter 12

Maximizing: The Ultimate Goal of Tiny House Lifestyle

Maximizing every nook and cranny of a tiny home can be a challenge. The idea is to make the house look bigger than the usual and make it appear homey, practical, and with ample elbow room.

Decorating a small home may be a challenge but it can be done. Here are tiny home decorating tips that you can use in your own home:

Create Focal Walls

The first impulse for a small space is to keep it clean and sleek to give an idea of space but here's an alternative choice: go bold with your design instead. You may have a corner area printed with bold color colors or use graphic wallpaper to liven up that corner area. Your focal wall can b anywhere you choose. Perhaps you have an entry zone near the door where you usually read the mails or probably you have a small dining table place near a corner window.

Paint a bold color or add an eye-catching element, like wallpaper, an artwork, or even a unique chair design. While there are no clear indications where a room ends and where it begins in a tiny home, you can still create the feeling of being alone with the décor you are going to use.

Mount Mirrors for Depth

Putting up a mirror to create an illusion of space is probably one of the oldest decorating tricks. A mirror can act as extra windows in your area and it can amplify the space. A position would be the entryway or anywhere where it can reflect an artwork or a nice view.

Some decorators would also suggest filling an entire wall with mirrors and then adding mirrored furniture to create an illusion of another room that is just not in full view. Putting colorful flowers and candles in strategic positions where the mirrors will reflect them make great décor alternatives.

If you don't want to put up giant mirrors, you may still create the same illusion by hanging a cluster of smaller mirrors. They don't have to be in the same size or they don't need to have matching designs, but you can create themes, such as all have rectangular shapes or round shapes or they can all have wood frames. The designs should be up to your taste and preference.

Lighten Up the Area

Don't think that if you have a smaller house you can't put decorations. You may opt to use clear objects because they take up little visual space so your small area won't look cramped. You may add a crystal chandelier; make sure the size is appropriate for the room. You can also use glass-top table with matching Lucite chairs, and then add in a mirror, and you end up brightening the area, thus, giving an illusion of a bigger room.

Swing-arm Sconces Free Up Some Space

If you cannot afford to include a side table for your living room, swing-arm sconces would be your best choice. You don't need a table for it, so that's a free space to work on. You can liven up a bare corner in your living room by installing swing-arm sconces. Most lighting shops offer these types of special lighting, so you can just ask a salesperson for assistance when you make your choices.

Open the Area Up

When you have a smaller area, expect to have smaller areas to work with. If you are scheduling your renovation soon, consider dividing the walls and replacing the partitions with interior glass doors. If you are only renting out the place, there's only so much that you can, so you may ask your landlord if you can take out a few doors in order to increase the natural flow of things and give the room some light.

Keep Every Area Clean and

Clutter Free

Even if you have a big area to work around, you need to keep your house clean and clutter free. Smaller spaces tend to look and feel cramped but if you keep all the rooms clean and orderly, and if you make sure the clutter has all been stacked out, it can make a lot of difference.

Use a Single Color Palette

When your home is small and there is too much going on in the design, no matter how clutter-free all the areas may be or how clean it can become, the house will still look cramped. Improve on the appearance of the house by using a single color palette because that will help pull everything together. It will also make the space look more expansive.

You can use two kinds of color and work with them.

Create Different Zones

If you live in a studio-type apartment and you don't have the luxury of having separate rooms, you can create "zones". Think about the things that you need to create a space for, like a place to sleep, to relax, to eat, or to cook. Then you establish separate areas for each of these activities.

You can create "rooms" with multiple seating areas, or you can use a curtained bed, or maybe build a window seat. You can also place a small table and chair, positioning is important if you want to create a bigger house illusion.

Use Multipurpose Furniture

Look for a table that can be used as a desk and dining table. Use deep sofas that can double as guest beds. You may also opt to just have a sofa-bed custom made, and you can ask the maker to add drawers under. Murphy beds would also be a great idea. For more free space, purchase folding chairs and collapsible tables. Remember that you don't need too many pieces if you have a smaller space to work with. The key is to choose furniture and decorative elements that offer maximum functionality without taking too much space.

Here are some Essential Tips that you can try to maximize your Space

- **Open your mind to different ideas.**

The fact that you're living in a small space gives you some right to do away with the conventional house decorating schemes! Go explore and find out what's best for you.

- **Furniture on wheels is a good option.**

You can move it around depending on your need for space in a certain area.

- **Invest on collapsible pieces.**

These items can give you what you need without taking your space all the time. You'll only have to deal with them as the need arises.

- **Look for any possible storage**.

It could be under your bed, the top of your closet or just behind the door.

Go for multifunctional items because it will save you so much on money and space. Instead of buying a bedside table, buy a bedside table with small drawers that you can use as storage.

- **Build high ceilings!**

Go for height if you can't go with length and maximize the aerial space.

- **Fill each corner to free up more space in the center**.

After all, you would not be able to use those wasted corners to much use anyway. Push back the furniture to the far end corners.

Opt for stacks instead of spread organizers since stacks would occupy mostly your vertical space.

- **Clear the clutter around each room.**

Remember to keep a regular schedule of clearing the clutter every time to ensure that there is enough space for the things that matter

- **Striking a balance in your house is the simplest way to maximize your space.**

Spread things equally around the house so that no space would look overly crowded.

- **Store occasional items and do not let them linger when they are not in use.**

They could block your pathway and as good as clutter when not in use.

- **Make a monthly house survey of the things you need and don't need**.

For instance, make a rule that things you haven't used for a year should be donated to charity or sold. This will keep your space tidy

- Make use of shelves, hooks, racks and organizers to maximize aerial, side and wall space.

- Use your closet ceilings to store rolls of papers or wrappers with the use of rubber bands pinned on top of your closet.

- The space under the stairs can be used as storage areas for your cleaning supplies such as brooms, dust bins, vacuum cleaners and rags. This will even make the stored items more accessible.

- Choose portability over bulkiness. Choose a portable DVD player, sewing machine or hair dryer. This will help you save space without missing anything.

- Have sofa beds in the living room that will serve as extra sleeping space in case you have an unexpected guest to accommodate. This will save you the space you should've allotted for an extra mattress!

- Add layers whenever possible. Add layers to your closet, book shelves, kitchen counter, etc. This will give you more utility and storage spaces.

- Opt for sliding doors/windows so that you won't need to worry about the space your door or window takes when they are opening or closing. By having sliding doors, you wouldn't need to worry about moving spaces near the door/window.

- Use room dividers instead of too much walls. Walls exist for division purposes which you could also accomplish by putting on draperies or much thinner dividers. Walls are thicker than dividers so they consume more space. Walls are also inflexible to bend to the demands of your space.

- Learn to fold your linens neatly so that it will take lesser closet or storage space.

- Minimize corners and add curves for better mobility around the house. Curves also allow you to cut on corner space.

- Add a loft whenever possible. You can add one in your room for an extra bed space or you can add a loft in the kitchen for supplies storage.

- Go for inflatables that you can just deflate and store when you don't need them, i.e. airbeds, air chairs, etc.

- Use portable ladders instead of stairs if possible because stairs can take too much space.

Keep in mind these space hacks for an easier tiny home living!

Chapter 13

__Essential Tips in Successful Tiny House Living__

Your place might be small, but it doesn't have to look small. Keep in mind that living in a tiny home is all about area management and tactical furniture arrangement and presentation

The following are some tips you can use to make sure that your tiny house would appear more spacious:

Be organized.

A small house that is well organized can look even more spacious than sloppy, chaotic big houses. The organized setting will give the impression that everything has been allotted ample space and that everything fits without looking cramped. This is also effective in maintaining a good traffic flow around the house despite the limited space since nothing out of place will be left strewn on the floor to block paths. Lastly, it will help you save precious time in looking for scattered items.

Use curtains that are the same color as the walls

Color blending is a very important step in creating an impression of a wider space. If you are planning to put on curtains, make sure that they are in the same color shade to create the illusion of unity and avoid color contrast.

Have an open source for natural light

Having a source for natural light serves two purposes: it helps you take advantage of daylight hence no electric charges, and it gives your house an open character unlike in areas where there are no windows or doors. It helps you breathe properly and it provides added warmth especially when the sunlight hits the room.

Bring outside colors inside

Remember what we told you about color blending and how it gives a unified and wider impression of the place? You need not limit yourself to the inside of your house! You can also blend your house's color with the outside surroundings. You need not make your house all green and brown; a simple huge mirror trick will do. Put an oversized mirror facing the door or window and it will reflect the surroundings from the inside. This will instantly give an impression of a wider space.

Put on the same color for adjacent spaces

Is your dining and living room placed in adjacent spaces? If so, make the flooring of both rooms in the same color, or at least try to stick in the same color shade/family. It will make the adjacent spaces look bigger as it will create wider boundaries.

Use neutral background and light colors

Light and neutral colors work wonders in making your space look more open and bare. This doesn't mean that you have to go all white in your house; of course you can put accents of different colors into it to make the place more tasteful. However, you need to make sure that the primary color surrounding the house is as light and bare as possible. Neutral, light brown hues are one of the best colors for the job.

Go for less furniture

If you have a tiny house, the first reflex you'll have is to shop for small furniture. Keep in mind that this is not always the best course of action to take. In a tiny home, less is always more.

Having smaller furniture could only be good if it has multiple functions – for example, an ottoman that could be used for storage, a TV rack with extra drawers and shelves. Go for bigger storage furniture instead. Also, if you have several small storage boxes because one can't handle everything you've got, the result will be too many small storage boxes scattered around the place. The fact that they're small boxes will not help you free up space. Here's what you need to do – choose less furniture that can accommodate everything that you need even if it means they are bigger. Having one large piece of furniture that can accomplish the job is better than having several small furniture pieces that serve only one purpose.

Add a floor-ceiling book shelf, but do not fill it

Aside from being a good focal point of the house, a floor-ceiling book shelf can push the wall and ceiling out to create an impression of a wider space. This will also serve as a good storage item for books, magazines and some art pieces. In putting books, keep in mind that you should not fill the entire book shelf. Leave some space empty and others filled. This will give the impression that there are a lot more spaces than you need. This will also make the shelf and its contents easier to look upon.

Avoid too much detail

Too much detail can create a feeling of

confusion around the house. This is because details compete for attention and it tends to make the space look smaller and divided. However, this doesn't mean that you should are forbidden to put any detail. If you must, put small details instead of large ones to make it blend to the space properly so that it won't compete for attention.

Have some large mirrors in the room

Oversized mirrors are your best friend when it comes to making your space look more spacious! Putting up a floor-to-ceiling mirror can immediately make your room look double in space. Try putting one in the smallest room you've got and you will surely see how much it works!

Use striped carpet

Just like it does with clothes, a stripe-designed carpet can make the flooring look longer or wider depending upon the type of stripes you have. Vertical stripes could make your flooring look longer, while horizontal stripes can make it look wider.

Schedule a décor display rotation

Say you have more things that your house can display without looking cramped; does it mean you get to store beautiful décor pieces for good? No it doesn't have to be like that. Putting all your décor pieces in your home all at the same time can make your tiny home look like a décor shop so avoid doing it.

What you can do instead is to come up

with a décor display rotation that will allow you to showcase your art pieces without crowding your house. You can do the décor display rotation by week, by month or whatever works for you! For instance, you can put on the glass figurines for a whole week while you store the little sculptures for display the following week. This could give you a chance to remodel your home and display your precious decors without making your space look small.

Examine the traffic flow

Making your tiny home look more spacious should not be left alone to the illusion eyes can play. It must also be felt by you and your guests.

What is crucial at this point is the traffic flow of your house. First, make an assessment of how traffic flow around the house currently is. Do you move around easily? If you're having a hard time moving around, chances are your house has a bad traffic flow.

There are several things you could do to improve your traffic flow. First, look at the corners of your home. Is there a wasted corner that can be adjusted to make the center more spacious? If there is, move your furniture farther up the corners until you feel the center of your home loosen up. Also try removing path blockers and clutter. If all else fails, try re-arranging the furniture.

There are some things around your house that you can use for many purposes. You'd be surprised to see how useful they can be while all this time you hated how much space they took up! Let's look at a large variety of item's that you can bring to use for MANY purposes!

- Silvery trays can be used to hold stationary on desks, makeup in the bathroom or cleaning supplies in the kitchen.

- Paper towel holders can also be used to store and showoff your bracelets and ribbon collection.
- CD racks can be used to store your container lids.
- Wine racks can be used to keep your spice bottles and tissue rolls on.
- Installing magazine racks inside cabinet doors can hold many things like foil rolls, craft papers, etc.
- If you have an empty wall, get creative and turn it into a photo wall!
- If you're less on cupboards, a great tip is to install wall shelves. Keep all the cute and decorative items up there on the shelf. This will look decorative and you can get a chance to show off your creativity! But keep it mind to clean these

shelves regularly as dust gathers on open items.

- Empty pill cases can also be used to store rings, spices, etc.

- Ice cube trays can hold many different items like earrings, rings,

- Tensions rods under the sink can hold your spray bottles.

- Sticking horizontal decorated tins on walls can hold many items and will also give a chic and creative effect!

- Mason jars or glass bottles can be used to store many things. Also, if you want to keep them on open shelves, you can decorate them using inspiration from some of these pictures:

Keeping the house clutter free

Now that your house is perfectly tidy and spotless now, you need to amend and re-think your cleaning routine to keep the house from getting jumbled up again and again. Small spaces somehow manage to get dirty and dusty very soon, so it's important to keep the house clean by using certain procedures.

Few chores to do daily:

This will help you keep the clutter monster at bay for good.

- Every morning, make a habit of making your bed immediately after waking up so that the room instantly looks tidy and orderly. A neat room will also prevent you from dumping in clutter like clothes and books!

- Before leaving a room, make sure you aren't leaving a mess behind and that everything is where it belongs.

- Now spend some time in your living room picking up clothes, books, papers, trash, shoes or any such thing that is littering the floor. Trash out any unwanted piled up junk.

- Dust furniture everyday as dusty furniture doesn't allow a clean room to look neat. The dust can also cause allergies to members of the family and can create infection.

- Mop the house regularly to keep the ceramic or laminated floors sparkly!

- Ventilate the washroom, change the towels, wipe off any water spills and use air fresheners regularly. You could also use scented candles, this can also look decorative and classy. Another option is to keep a bowl of baking soda in any corner of the room to absorb the foul smell in your toilet.

- Clean your kitchen up, pick up all the unnecessary things lying around the kitchen counters and keep them back in their places.

- Prepare all your ingredients before you start cooking to help you stay relaxed while you're preparing the food.

- Clean up the counters while you cook and wash dishes, pots and utensils you use right away instead of piling them up in the sink.

- Clean up any spills weather they are on your stove top, in your oven, on the floor or on the kitchen island. It is easier to get rid of the stains when they're fresh.

- Boil some baking soda in a bowl of water and pour it in the sink. Let sit and pour some vinegar, it will wash down any built up residue in the drainage pipe.

- Sweep the kitchen once you're done with dinner and dishes.
- Wipe all the mirrors, bathtubs, showers and sinks. Regularly change your washcloths, towels, bedsheets, pillowcases, etc to keep them completely spotless.
- Sort out your bills! Keep aside the paid ones, keep the pending bills in view as to prevent overdue bills.
- Wipe your windows, window sills and all the doors.
- Take out the trash every night.

Putting in some effort on a weekly basis will keep you tension free for a long time! Follow this routine on daily basis and trust me, you won't have to worry about decluttering the house again!

Few weekly chores:

Some weekly tasks to add to your schedule will help to maintain the house well. Such as,

- Vacuum your entire house once a week and dust all the lamps, frames, bookshelves, electronics and ceiling light fixtures thoroughly about twice or thrice a week.
- Wipe all the kitchen cabinets, drawers and other furniture with clean washcloths.
- Clean the space inside your oven and your stove top and make it spotless.
- Wipe the microwave and other kitchen appliances.
- Clear clutter in your fridge, toss out any open packs that haven't

been used since one week and arrange everything in it's proper place.

- Change the bedsheets, pillowcases, duvet covers and towels.
- Use a hand vacuum to clean the sofas and the space between them.
- Clean the bathrooms properly, using your favorite cleaning products!

A monthly cleaning schedule:

To make your spring cleaning easier, put in some extra effort every month and clear up the hidden dust and throw out anything that is no more required for you and your family.

- The most important area that requires your attention at this time is your refrigerator. Throw out any expired food, clean up spills and spread cling wrap on your shelves if you haven't already done that before.

- Change your hood's filter and wipe off any sticky and greasy stain on your backsplash.

- Second most important job is to scrub the grouts. If ignored, a lot of dirt will collect and settle in the grouts ruining the look of your entire house. Make a paste of baking soda and hot boiling water, pour this all over your grouts and let sit for one hour. Then pour vinegar over it and scrub the area with a grout scrub. Ta-Da! You just got back your spotless and brand-new like flooring again!

- Then, dust all the show pieces, stand fans, ceiling fans and telephones.

- Vacuum window sills and hard to reach areas such as behind the sofa, bed, etc.

Even after all this hard work, there are some tasks that need your attention such as inside the pantry or the fireplace. That can wait until spring cleaning!

Spring cleaning

Your spring cleaning has surely become easier now! So check out this schedule and start away!

Start with your bedroom,

- Sort out your closet and keep away all the warm winter wear as you won't need them anymore.
- Wash pillows and mattress covers and flip your mattress every six months to increase its life.
- Vacuum the mattress, the area around the bed and any rugs in your room.

- Change the batteries on your wall clock.
- Wipe the lamps, lights and chandelier properly.
- Vacuum all the carpets and rugs around the house.
-

Moving onto the living room,

- Wash your sofa covers. If you have leathers sofas, wipe them thoroughly.
- Clean up your fireplace and heaters.
- Take out books from your bookshelf, dust them and rotate them and keep them back to prevent them from warping.
- Dust the blinds or if you have curtains, take them down and send them to the laundry.
- Wash all the cushions

Now, pull yourself together before moving to the biggest job. Yes, the kitchen!

- Replace the baking soda in your fridge and freezer.
- Discard any expired food there.
- Wipe the fridge from inside and outside.
- Wipe your kitchen walls and ceiling lights.
- Polish all the silverware.
- Wipe your hanging pot rack and polish the copper.
- Clean the inside of your cabinets and pantry and make sure nothing unnecessary is lying around.

Get your family to participate in the spring cleaning! This can then become a family project and everyone can bond with each other as they will be spending quite a lot of time together. Make a schedule for the cleaning by checking when each member of the family is committed to a plan.

Keeping the clutter at bay

To keep the clutter from entering your house, you could try following these simple rules.

- Before buying anything, think about where you will keep it. Unless you come up with an appropriate place, do NOT buy it! If you do so, then get ready to face another project of decluttering the house.

- If you do buy something, remove something from the house. Either donate it, sell it or throw it. For example, you see this perfectly fantastic pair of jeans you are in love with. If you go ahead with buying the product, make sure you remove another pair of clothing, or any other item from the house. This habit will help you from spending too much money and will keep the clutter away.

- Don't subscribe for magazines and newsletter, they lie around the house for a long time before you even take notice of it. Instead, be environment friendly and just read them online.

- Keep a paper shredder near the front door and in the home office. Shred the junk papers immediately so they won't get misplaced and will reduce the clutter.

Conclusion

Take your time working through these tips. Some of them are easier to implement than others and that's going to prove even more important when you're working on putting them into action. If you like some of them better than others that's great too. Just take a little time to do them. You're going to be very impressed and happy that your entire house looks less cluttered. Plus, you're going to have the added benefit of actually being able to find the things that you want and need in your home.

Adding more storage to your home really isn't difficult at all. What you need to do is consider each room as a separate space and think about what you need to store there or what you might be able to store there in the future. There are so many ways to make the most of any spaces that you have and so often people will overlook them, like overlooking the space under the stairs in your home. This space is valuable and it's going to increase the size of your storage space by a lot.

■∙∙■

Made in United States
Orlando, FL
19 June 2023